Sacred Salutations

a thirty-day journey to a
new conversation with your life

Andrenee Boothe

DIVINE HOUSE
B O O K S

©2016 Printed in the United States of America

ISBN # 978-1-5323-2719-3

Sacred Salutations

A Thirty-Day Journey
To a New Conversation with Your Life!

Andrenee Boothe

This book is dedicated to every woman that reads it!
You are me and I am You!

I love You!

FOREWORD

I am celebrating this beautifully amazing "literary offspring" of my daughter in Spirit and Divine Life. The simplistically profound words that are spoken forth from her mind will bless you indeed. I know so..

Within everyone of us is an inner conversation; a rhythm of imagination and thought that establishes our perception of Life and Self. As we continue to "speak to ourselves," we find that the pictures of our lives begin to reflect and mirror the reality of our thoughts and conversation. We find ourselves "becoming what we conversation about," emotionally and mentally, in every moment of day. We either build ourselves or destroy ourselves, by the rhythms of our silent hearts.

Andrenee has beautifully crafted a "pathway of conversation" for the reader; beauty sparks that will inspire and awaken an original groove on the inside. And when this "groove" is divinely embraced, it will establish a new picture of YOU, on the outside..

Undrai Fizer, publisher

Table of Contents

Table of Contents

SACRED SALUTATIONS

Sacred Salutations is an invitation to a thirty-day journey of greetings that assist You in developing an intentional pattern of beginning Your day with healthy conversations with Yourself. You are Your first lover. Everything starts and ends with You.

A Salutation is an expression of greeting, goodwill, or courtesy by word, gesture, or ceremony. The word or phrase of greeting (as Gentlemen or Dear Sir or Madam) that conventionally comes immediately before the body of a letter.

You are the first and last person that You greet every day. Your uprisings and down-settings are absolutely sacred. Honor Your existence by starting and ending Your day properly. How You salute Yourself will determine how Life will respond to You.

Each day is a fresh start. No matter what may have happened the day before, it is no longer real. The past is just a memory. The only time You have is now.

Your life is Sacred. Period. Sacred moments are not only limited to when You go to church, when You pray, when You fast, or when You meditate. Everything about You is Sacred. All of Your experiences, memories, failures, triumphs, highs and lows. Everything! May I invite You at this very moment to just begin to give thanks for all that has happened in Your life up until now. Everything that has happened in Your life before right now has led to You this book. Even if how You received this book may appear to have been by accident, believe me, it wasn't. It means You are ready to have a new conversation with Yourself.

YOUR THOUGHTS

You live in a world that began with a thought. The Mind of God is the beginning of all things. As a result, You are an idea (thought) from the Mind of God. (Take a few minutes to think about these three statements)

According to the Laboratory of Neuro Imaging at the University of Southern California, the average person has about 48.6 thoughts per minute. That adds up to a total of 70,000 thoughts per day.

Because You live in a thought world where everyone around You is thinking, You will always be introduced to many different thoughts and ideas. In other words, thoughts come and go throughout Your mind moment by moment.

The average person is not aware of their thought life. Most of us are more aware of what is going on outside of us. If we pay more attention to what is going on outside of us, we will only be inclined to want to fix what is happening from the outside. Everything that happens outside of us is only the effect of our thoughts, not the cause. This is why fixing the effect does not solve anything. It may ease the problem temporarily, but give it a little bit of time and I guarantee You it will resurface again. Gone are the days of a temporary fix. Now is the time to look within.

You were made in the image and likeness of God. You were created to be a thinker. Your thoughts help You to create pictures in Your mind. Pictures are developed by a focused thought. Just like a camera, a clear picture requires a focused lens.

Did You know that You have control over Your thoughts? I know that seems overwhelming, especially since we are bombarded with so many thoughts a day, but I promise You it is possible. All it requires is awareness and intention. Pay attention to Yourself. Pay attention to Your feelings. Your feelings are Your friends. They are there to let You know if You have been thinking a thought repeatedly. For example, You are planning for Your vacation in the Bahamas, and then all of sudden You start to feel excited. Those feelings of excitement are a result of You thinking about how about much fun You are going to have.

Imagine what Your life would be like if You made a conscious decision to monitor Your thoughts so that You can change the old thoughts for new ones?

YOUR BELIEFS

A belief is the state of mind in which a person thinks something to be the case, with or without there being empirical evidence to prove that something is the case with factual certainty.

Abraham Hicks defines belief as this: "A belief is a thought that You keep on thinking".

Your beliefs play a huge part in Your decision making. Your beliefs also play a huge part in how You see Yourself and the world.

"We don't believe the world we see; we see the world we believe".

We all believe in something. Our beliefs shape who we are and reveal the things that we value. Every human being has a belief system that they use and it is through this method that we understand the world around us. Our belief systems can be compared to computer operating systems. With technology advancing at a high-speed rate, ever so often there is a new update to a computer operating system which is supposed to make the computer function better and/or easier. This same principle can be applied to the exchange of old beliefs with new ones. When a new idea or new experience comes along, we have the option to rid ourselves of a particular belief so that we can live and lead better lives.

However, more often times than none, this is not the case. Many of us are still walking around with belief systems that are as old as our great, great, great, great, great, great grandparents. As a result, each generation repeats what the prior generation did. I believe this is what we refer to as "generational curses". But I have great news!!!! The "curse" can be reversed!!

All it takes is Your willingness to let go of a belief. That's it. No exorcism. No prayer lines. No magic potion. No manipulation. If the belief no longer serves You, just let it go!

INNER CONVERSATIONS

A conversation is the informal exchange of ideas by spoken words. There is always an internal conversation going on inside of us, even when we are not paying attention. In this conversation, there is always one voice that is louder. This voice is the one that You listen to the most. Unfortunately, sometimes, the voice we listen to is not the voice of our Higher Self (God), but I guarantee You this thirty-day journey will be the catalyst to inclining Your ear to the voice of God.

Do You know that the Universe is listening to the conversations that You have with Yourself? The universe is designed to work with You. The universe is on Your side. Whatever You desire or ask for, there are universal laws in place to grant Your request.

Observe Your surroundings right now. Take a quick look at Your life. Whether You believe it or not, You asked for this. Take a breath. This is wonderful news!

We are naturally creatures of habit. I believe we were intentionally created this way. What is a habit? A habit is a settled or regular tendency or practice/routine. The Universe responds to the rhythm of Your life. The rhythm of Your Life is a compilation of Your thoughts, conversations, emotions and decisions. The rhythm of Your life begins with a conversation.

A lot of our internal dialogue usually consists of what others have said to or about us over the years. It's like a record with a scratch on it and it repeats itself over and over and over again. Ever wonder why life seems to repeat itself? You feel like You are experiencing the same scenarios, and sometimes even at the same time of the year? You have tried endlessly to change friends, change hairstyles, change jobs, or even change Your location, yet nothing really changes? This is life's way of saying it is time for a new conversation with Yourself.

A new conversation consists of new thoughts and new thoughts overtime become new beliefs. This is going to require some effort on Your part. You have to be open and willing to introduce Yourself to something new. It may feel uncomfortable in the beginning, but I promise You, if You stay committed to this journey, every day it will get easier and easier because there will be less resistance.

Are You ready? Let's get it on!

DAY 1

Good Morning Beautiful!

How are You feeling today?
(Take a Deep Breath in, and a Deep Breath out)
Do You know how much I love You?
I love You more than You can ever imagine.
- Just look at You -
Your eyes, Your nose, Your lips, Your hips and Your face,
They are just marvelous!
My darling there is none like You in the Earth.
There is nothing but goodness awaiting You today.
May You see, taste and feel this goodness as it is
Yours for the receiving!
Enjoy!

Take a few minutes to remember a moment in Your life when You felt the most beautiful. If perhaps You are having trouble remembering, use Your imagination to picture Yourself feeling beautiful. Stay there until it feels really good.

Gratitude Journal

Write three things that You are grateful for and why:
(You can write more if You want)

_____

_____

_____

_____

_____

_____

_____

_____

_____

_____

_____

_____

_____

_____

_____

_____

_____

_____

_____

_____

_____

_____

_____

_____

_____

_____

_____

_____

DAY 2

Good Morning Magnificence!

What an awesome time it is to be alive!
(Take a Deep Breath in; take a Deep Breath out)
The world is awaiting Your arrival,
So, You cannot afford to be late.
You possess all of the splendor and awe that was present at the
very beginning of time.
May each step You take today be an expression
of brilliance and elegance!
Enjoy!

Take a few minutes to remember a moment in Your life when
You felt the most magnificent. If perhaps You are having
trouble remembering, use Your imagination to picture Yourself
feeling magnificent. Stay there until it feels really good.

Gratitude Journal

Write three things that You are grateful for and why:
(You can write more if You want)

_____

_____

_____

_____

_____

_____

_____

_____

_____

_____

_____

_____

_____

_____

_____

_____

_____

_____

_____

_____

_____

_____

_____

_____

DAY 3

Good Morning Fabulous!

It's a new day!
(Take a Deep Breath in; take a Deep Breath out)
What shall we encounter today?
Joy, Peace, Harmony, and of course Love!
How do I know this?
All of these are in You like a well springing up into
everlasting life.
Get Your buckets ready to draw from this abundant supply,
And don't forget to share from Your bounty of goodness,
There's more than enough to give and still have left over!

Take a few minutes to remember a moment in Your life when
You felt the most fabulous. If perhaps You are having trouble
remembering, use Your imagination to picture Yourself feeling
fabulous. Stay there until it feels really good.

Gratitude Journal

Write three things that You are grateful for and why:
(You can write more if You want)

_____

_____

_____

_____

_____

_____

_____

_____

_____

_____

_____

_____

_____

_____

_____

_____

_____

_____

_____

_____

_____

_____

_____

_____

_____

_____

_____

_____

_____

_____

_____

_____

_____

_____

_____

_____

_____

_____

_____

_____

Day 4

Good Morning Diva!

This is the day that the Lord has made and it belongs to You!
(Take a Deep Breath in; take a Deep Breath out)
You call the shots,
Choose Your experiences like You would choose a pair of shoes.
Let Your choices be the perfect color coordination
with Your vision,
Unapologetically,
No permission needed,
All rights reserved,
Let's do this!

Take a few minutes to remember a moment in Your life
when You felt like a diva. If perhaps You are having trouble
remembering, use Your imagination to picture Yourself feeling
like a diva. Stay there until it feels really good.

Gratitude Journal

Write three things that You are grateful for and why:
(You can write more if You want)

_____

_____

_____

_____

_____

_____

_____

_____

_____

_____

_____

_____

DAY 5

Good Morning Phenomenon!

A phenomenon is known to be anything which manifests itself,
In other words,
You were meant to be seen and marveled,
(Take a Deep Breath in; take a Deep Breath out)
As You walk out of Your home,
And allow Your feet to touch the pavement,
May each step say out loud,
"I am here!"
Loud enough for the trees and the birds to hear it!
You have exactly what this world needs,
Please be guided accordingly!

Take a few minutes to remember a moment in Your life when
You felt phenomenal. If perhaps You are having trouble
remembering, use Your imagination to picture Yourself feeling
phenomenal. Stay there until it feels really good.

Gratitude Journal

Write three things that You are grateful for and why:
(You can write more if You want)

_____

_____

_____

_____

_____

_____

_____

_____

_____

_____

_____

_____

_____

_____

_____

_____

_____

_____

_____

_____

_____

_____

_____

_____

_____

_____

Day 6

Good Morning Wonderful!

You have an Awe-Spiring day ahead of You!
(Take a Deep Breath in; take a Deep Breath out)
A day full of wonder!
Today Your eyes will be opened,
And You are going to find the keys You needed!
You are going to unlock a plethora of hidden treasures!
SO, give away what You no longer need,
And make room for what is to come!

Take a few minutes to remember a moment in Your life when
You felt Your most wonderful. If perhaps You are having
trouble remembering, use Your imagination to picture Yourself
feeling wonderful. Stay there until it feels really good.

Gratitude Journal

Write three things that You are grateful for and why:
(You can write more if You want)

_____

_____

_____

_____

_____

_____

_____

_____

_____

_____

_____

_____

_____

_____

_____

_____

_____

_____

_____

_____

_____

_____

_____

_____

_____

_____

DAY 7

Good Morning Sexy!

Your body is a Wonderland!
Every single part of You screams Sexy!
(Take a Deep Breath in; take a Deep Breath out)
Examine every curve of Your body in the mirror and repeat
these words out Loud:
"I am Perfect, Whole, Complete and Sexy too!"
In this moment love Your body like there were no expectations
of it to look a certain way,
Love it like You had nothing to compare it to,
Love it like it You are aware that it is the very thing that
protected all of Your major organs,
And,
Let's make a promise to be eternally grateful for this
magnificent body that serves as the temple,
That covers and protects Your soul.

Take a few minutes to remember a moment in Your life
when You felt really sexy. If perhaps You are having trouble
remembering, use Your imagination to picture Yourself feeling
sexy. Stay there until it feels really good.

Gratitude Journal

Write three things that You are grateful for and why:
(You can write more if You want)

_____

_____

_____

_____

_____

_____

_____

_____

_____

_____

_____

_____

DAY 8

Good Morning Gorgeous!

Today has Your name all over it!!
(Take a Deep Breath in; take a Deep Breath out)
All that belongs to You is coming Your way,
No need to fret or worry,
The path has been set before You and the ways have been
straightened,
Just walk therein,
Your steps are ordered,
Walk with boldness and confidence!
I mean,
You are gorgeous honey, You couldn't walk any other way,
Go and get Yours!

Take a few minutes to remember a moment in Your life
when You felt gorgeous. If perhaps You are having trouble
remembering, use Your imagination to picture Yourself feeling
gorgeous. Stay there until it feels really good.

Gratitude Journal

Write three things that You are grateful for and why:
(You can write more if You want)

_____

_____

_____

_____

_____

_____

_____

_____

_____

_____

_____

_____

_____

DAY 9

Good Morning Goddess!

Remember love, You are an idea from the Mind of God!
You are in a class of Gods!
How does that make You feel?
(Take a Deep Breath in, and a Deep Breath out)
Doesn't that feel good? (I knew it would)
Now what shall we create today?
There is no need to be intimidated by any form of chaos.
Chaos is only an opportunity for You to strategize and call
things back into order!
Let the festivities begin!

Take a few minutes to remember a moment in Your life when
You felt like a goddess. If perhaps You are having trouble
remembering, use Your imagination to picture Yourself feeling
like a goddess. Stay there until it feels really good.

Gratitude Journal

Write three things that You are grateful for and why:
(You can write more if You want)

_____

_____

_____

_____

_____

_____

_____

_____

_____

_____

_____

_____

_____

_____

_____

_____

_____

_____

_____

_____

_____

_____

_____

DAY 10

Good Morning Queen!

Welcome to Your World!
(Take a Deep Breath in; take a Deep Breath out)
Everything at this very moment is under Your rule and
jurisdiction,
You are wired to command where You stand,
You shall Decree a Thing and it shall be established for You,
And the Light of God will shine in Your ways,
You don't have to fear this Responsibility.
The fact that You are here,
Right now,
Is proof that You are ready to reign in Your Kingdom,
And it is So!

Take a few minutes to remember a moment in Your life when
You felt like a queen. If perhaps You are having trouble
remembering, use Your imagination to picture Yourself feeling
like a queen. Stay there until it feels really good.

Gratitude Journal

Write three things that You are grateful for and why:
(You can write more if You want)

_____

_____

_____

_____

_____

_____

_____

_____

_____

_____

_____

_____

DAY 11

Good Morning Gem!

Do You know how valuable You are?
You cannot be bought!
(Take a Deep Breath in; take a Deep Breath out)
Within You is an immeasurable treasure,
That can and will sustain You,
And all of the Generations that follow You,
Your worth is far above rubies,
Handle Yourself with Care and Patience,
Your life depends on it!

Take a few minutes to remember a moment in Your life when
You felt the most valuable. If perhaps You are having trouble
remembering, use Your imagination to picture Yourself feeling
valuable. Stay there until it feels really good.

Gratitude Journal

Write three things that You are grateful for and why:
(You can write more if You want)

_____

_____

_____

_____

_____

_____

_____

_____

_____

_____

_____

_____

DAY 12

Good Morning Excellence!

How Excellent You are in the Earth!
(Take a Deep Breath in; take a Deep Breath out)
You were made perfectly!
You are a masterpiece!
Designed to be the Glory of God in the Earth,
The same creative power used to organize the planets, the
moon and the stars
Is the same power that created You!
You are a perfect fit for this planet.
Now go ahead and be Excellent!

Take a few minutes to remember a moment in Your life when
You felt the most excellent. If perhaps You are having trouble
remembering, use Your imagination to picture Yourself feeling
excellent. Stay there until it feels really good.

Gratitude Journal

Write three things that You are grateful for and why:
(You can write more if You want)

_____

_____

_____

_____

_____

_____

_____

_____

_____

_____

_____

_____

_____

_____

_____

_____

_____

_____

_____

_____

_____

_____

_____

_____

_____

_____

DAY 13

Good Morning Joy!

Joy is Your birthright!
Joy isn't something You have to ask permission for,
(Take a Deep Breath in; take a Deep Breath out)
It's available to You and it is within reach,
With every waking second,
Whether You are thinking about it or not.
It's that bubbly feeling,
That You experience,
For absolutely no particular reason.
Like what You are feeling right now,
Now stay right there. . . .
For as long as You want to!

Take a few minutes to remember a moment in Your life when
You felt the most joyful. If perhaps You are having trouble
remembering, use Your imagination to picture Yourself feeling
joyful. Stay there until it feels really good.

Gratitude Journal

Write three things that You are grateful for and why:
(You can write more if You want)

_____

_____

_____

_____

_____

_____

_____

_____

_____

_____

_____

_____

DAY 14

Good Morning Peace!

Peace is only a breath away!
(Take a Deep Breath in; take a Deep Breath out)
Its existence is not incumbent upon whether You can pay Your
rent or not,
The current balance in Your bank account,
Or a diagnosis from Your doctor,
Peace is,
Knowing that all is well,
Even when the storms of life are raging,
It's a choice,
And I know You will choose wisely,
Be at Peace!

Take a few minutes to remember a moment in Your life when
You felt the most peaceful. If perhaps You are having trouble
remembering, use Your imagination to picture Yourself feeling
peaceful. Stay there until it feels really good.

Gratitude Journal

Write three things that You are grateful for and why:
(You can write more if You want)

_____

_____

_____

_____

_____

_____

_____

_____

_____

_____

_____

_____

_____

DAY 15

Good Morning Hope!

You are Here!
And the good news is Hope has not retired neither
has she lost her job!
She is always at her post and waiting for Your arrival!
(Take a Deep Breath in; take a Deep Breath out)
She's looking You right in the face,
Cheering You on,
She is Your most faithful Audience,
Always ready to give You a standing Ovation,
Let this Day be Your Best Performance…
Hope awaits You!

Take a few minutes to remember a moment in Your life when
You felt the most hopeful. If perhaps You are having trouble
remembering, use Your imagination to picture Yourself feeling
hopeful. Stay there until it feels really good.

Gratitude Journal

Write three things that You are grateful for and why:
(You can write more if You want)

_____

_____

_____

_____

_____

_____

_____

_____

_____

_____

_____

_____

_____

DAY 16

Good Morning Rockstar!

You are the Most famous person in Your World!
(Take a Deep Breath in; take a Deep Breath out)
There is no one more important than You right now!
You have what the World needs!
You cannot afford not to show up…
Walk this way,
Talk this way,
Live this way,
Be this way,
You Rock lady!!

Take a few minutes to remember a moment in Your life when
You felt like a Rockstar. If perhaps You are having trouble
remembering, use Your imagination to picture Yourself feeling
like a Rockstar. Stay there until it feels really good.

Gratitude Journal

Write three things that You are grateful for and why:
(You can write more if You want)

_____

_____

_____

_____

_____

_____

_____

_____

_____

_____

_____

_____

_____

_____

_____

_____

_____

_____

_____

_____

_____

_____

_____

_____

_____

_____

_____

_____

DAY 17

Good Morning Powerhouse!

Look all around You,
Look at what You have created!
You are Powerful!
(Take a Deep Breath in; take a Deep Breath out)
And if there is anything around You that You no longer desire,
You can use the same Power to turn things around,
In Your favor,
And if You gave Your power away,
You can reclaim it!
Right Now!
It's in Your Hands!

Take a few minutes to remember a moment in Your life when You felt the most powerful. If perhaps You are having trouble remembering, use Your imagination to picture Yourself feeling powerful. Stay there until it feels really good.

Gratitude Journal

Write three things that You are grateful for and why:
(You can write more if You want)

_____

_____

_____

_____

_____

_____

_____

_____

_____

_____

_____

_____

_____

_____

_____

_____

_____

_____

_____

_____

_____

_____

_____

_____

_____

SACRED SALUTATIONS

DAY 18

Good Morning Dreamer!

Your Imagination is Your SuperPower!
(Take a Deep Breath in; take a Deep Breath out)
If You Can Dream it, You can Achieve it!
However You see Yourself when lost in Your Daydreams,
Is the Person You were meant to Be,
It may not happen overnight,
But best believe,
It's going to happen!
Keep on Dreaming and Keep on Living!
I Dare You to!

Take a few minutes to remember a moment in Your life when You felt like You could achieve all of Your dreams. If perhaps You are having trouble remembering, use Your imagination to picture Yourself achieving all of Your dreams. Stay there until it feels really good.

Gratitude Journal

Write three things that You are grateful for and why:
(You can write more if You want)

_____

_____

_____

_____

_____

_____

_____

_____

_____

_____

_____

_____

_____

DAY 19

Good Morning Friend!

You are Your Sister's keeper,
There is no separation,
When You Win, she wins; when she loses, You lose,
(Take a Deep Breath in; take a Deep Breath out)
Your Sister is You,
So, let's all win together,
Even if it means we have let each other go,
For a period of time,
Things are always working together,
For the Greater Good!

Take a few minutes to remember a moment in Your life when
You felt like a great friend. If perhaps You are having trouble
remembering, use Your imagination to picture Yourself being a
great friend. Stay there until it feels really good.

Gratitude Journal

Write three things that You are grateful for and why:
(You can write more if You want)

_____

_____

_____

_____

_____

_____

_____

_____

_____

_____

_____

_____

DAY 20

Good Morning Prophetess!

Your Words have Power!
(Take a Deep Breath in; take a Deep Breath out)
When You speak the Earth responds!
Let the words of Your mouth,
And meditation the of Your heart,
Be in agreement with the Vision that You have for Your life,
Heaven is waiting for Your invitation,
To unlock all that belongs to You
What shall we declare today?

Take a few minutes to remember a moment in Your life when You felt like Your words had power. If perhaps You are having trouble remembering, use Your imagination to picture Yourself speaking things that You desired and seeing them come to pass. Stay there until it feels really good.

Gratitude Journal

Write three things that You are grateful for and why:
(You can write more if You want)

_____

_____

_____

_____

_____

_____

_____

_____

_____

_____

_____

DAY 21

Good Morning Visionary!

I see You sitting on Top of the world!
I see You dancing like no one is watching!
I see You!!
(Take a Deep Breath in; take a Deep Breath out)
I see You surrounded by a love, joy and a peace that surpasses
all understanding,
I see You perfect whole and complete!
I see You with all Power in Your hand,
I see You!!
What Do You See?

Take a few minutes to remember a moment in Your life when
You felt like a visionary. If perhaps You are having trouble
remembering, use Your imagination to picture Yourself living
out Your vision. Stay there until it feels really good.

Gratitude Journal

Write three things that You are grateful for and why:
(You can write more if You want)

_____

_____

_____

_____

_____

_____

_____

_____

_____

_____

_____

_____

_____

_____

_____

_____

_____

_____

_____

_____

_____

_____

_____

_____

_____

_____

_____

DAY 22

Good Morning Priestess!!

You are seated at the Right Hand of God!
(Take a Deep Breath in; take a Deep Breath out)
You represent wisdom, serenity, knowledge and understanding!
Trust Your femininity,
For in it lies the path to Your intuition,
And Your intuition assists You with becoming more in touch
with Your first mind,
So, if ever You feel out of touch with the truth,
Remember within You lies the power to redeem Yourself,
Back to who You know You truly are!

Take a few minutes to remember a moment in Your life
when You forgave Yourself. If perhaps You are having trouble
remembering, use Your imagination to picture Yourself
forgiving Yourself for everything. Stay there until it
feels really good.

Gratitude Journal

Write three things that You are grateful for and why:
(You can write more if You want)

_____

_____

_____

_____

_____

_____

_____

_____

_____

_____

_____

_____

DAY 23

Good Morning Sunshine!

You are the Light of the World!
(Take a Deep Breath in; take a Deep Breath out)
Shine bright like the Sun.
Let no-one or no-thing dim Your light.
If You encounter darkness today,
Do not run from it,
For it is not real.
It is only absent of Your Presence,
So, on this Beautiful day,
Let there be You!

Take a few minutes to remember a moment in Your life when
You felt like You were a light in a dark moment. If perhaps
You are having trouble remembering, use Your imagination to
picture Yourself being a light to someone's darkness. Stay there
until it feels really good.

Gratitude Journal

Write three things that You are grateful for and why:
(You can write more if You want)

_____

_____

_____

_____

_____

_____

_____

_____

_____

_____

_____

_____

_____

_____

_____

_____

_____

_____

_____

_____

_____

_____

_____

_____

_____

_____

_____

_____

_____

_____

_____

_____

_____

_____

_____

_____

_____

_____

DAY 24

Good Morning Champion!

You are fighting a good fight,
You are keeping the faith,
Take a bow!
(Take a Deep Breath in; take a Deep Breath out)
Keep running the race,
Stay focused,
Look neither to left nor to the right,
It's a fixed fight,
You have already WON!!

Take a few minutes to remember a moment in Your life when You felt like a champion. If perhaps You are having trouble remembering, use Your imagination to picture Yourself being a champion. Stay there until it feels really good.

Gratitude Journal

Write three things that You are grateful for and why:
(You can write more if You want)

_____

_____

_____

_____

_____

_____

_____

_____

_____

_____

_____

DAY 25

Good Morning Fearless!

You are love personified!
(Take a Deep Breath in; take a Deep Breath out)
What if nothing bad could ever happen to You?
What if You are loved beyond Your wildest dreams?
What if it's impossible for anyone or anything to hurt You?
What if everything You have ever dreamed of is
Yours for the taking?
So go on ahead and forgive quickly,
Open up Your heart again,
Take a chance on Yourself,
You already know the answers to those questions,
No more delay!

Take a few minutes to remember a moment in Your life when
You felt the most fearless. If perhaps You are having trouble
remembering, use Your imagination to picture Yourself being
fearless. Stay there until it feels really good.

Gratitude Journal

Write three things that You are grateful for and why:
(You can write more if You want)

_____

_____

_____

_____

_____

_____

_____

_____

_____

_____

_____

DAY 26

Good Morning Conqueror!

You are more than a Conqueror!
(Take a Deep Breath in; take a Deep Breath out)
There is nothing that You cannot overcome,
Don't tell Your God about Your Mountains,
Tell Your mountains about Your God,
Is there anything too hard for the Lord?
Not one thing!
So, crush Your giants today,
Until they become like ants!
Now with that being said,
What shall we conquer today?

Take a few minutes to remember a moment in Your life when
You felt like You conquered something. If perhaps You are
having trouble remembering, use Your imagination to picture
Yourself conquering something You have been trying to
conquer for a long time. Stay there until it feels really good.

Gratitude Journal

Write three things that You are grateful for and why:
(You can write more if You want)

_____

_____

_____

_____

_____

_____

_____

_____

_____

_____

_____

Day 27

Good Morning Grace!

You are the epitome of Elegance!
(Take a Deep Breath in; take a Deep Breath out)
You are Delicate,
Yet You are so Powerful,
You are Peaceful,
Yet Your Presence speaks Volumes,
You are Simple,
Yet Your Life is So Profound,
A Complicated Mystery,
Waiting to be Revealed!

Take a few minutes to remember a moment in Your life when
You felt the most graceful. If perhaps You are having trouble
remembering, use Your imagination to picture Yourself feeling
graceful. Stay there until it feels really good.

Gratitude Journal

Write three things that You are grateful for and why:
(You can write more if You want)

_____

_____

_____

_____

_____

_____

_____

_____

_____

_____

_____

Day 28

Good Morning Angel!

Are You Ready to Spread Your Wings?
(Take a Deep Breath in; take a Deep Breath out)
Someone is in Need of You today.
You have the Solution,
To a reoccurring problem,
You have the Answer,
To a troubling question,
You have a message,
That only You can deliver,
What are You waiting for?
It's time to fly!

Take a few minutes to remember a moment in Your life when
You felt like an angel. If perhaps You are having trouble
remembering, use Your imagination to picture Yourself being
an angel. Stay there until it feels really good.

Gratitude Journal

Write three things that You are grateful for and why:
(You can write more if You want)

_____

_____

_____

_____

_____

_____

_____

_____

_____

_____

_____

DAY 29

Good Morning Prosperity!

Your cup is full and running over!
(Take a Deep Breath in; take a Deep Breath out)
Heaven's bounty is at your fingertips,
Withdrawals are endless,
Happiness and Wealth shall forever be your portion,
Lack is only an illusion,
You were made to flourish and to thrive.
Give and it will return to you a hundredfold!

Take a few minutes to remember a moment in Your life when
You felt the most prosperous. If perhaps You are having
trouble remembering, use Your imagination to picture Yourself
feeling prosperous. Stay there until it feels really good.

Gratitude Journal

Write three things that You are grateful for and why:
(You can write more if You want)

_____

_____

_____

_____

_____

_____

_____

_____

_____

_____

_____

_____

_____

_____

_____

_____

_____

_____

_____

_____

_____

_____

_____

_____

_____

DAY 30

Good Morning Freedom!

You are as Free as You think You are!
(Take a Deep Breath in; take a Deep Breath out)
There are no limits,
There are no boundaries,
You just have to master this game called "Life",
And have lots of fun while You're at it.
Allow this Freedom,
To take You where no man has gone before,
Explore, Discover, Create,
And be Free!

Take a few minutes to remember a moment in Your life
when You felt Your freest. If perhaps You are having trouble
remembering, use Your imagination to picture Yourself feeling
free. Stay there until it feels really good.

Gratitude Journal

Write three things that You are grateful for and why:
(You can write more if You want)

_____

_____

_____

_____

_____

_____

_____

_____

_____

_____

_____

_____

_____

_____

_____

_____

_____

_____

_____

_____

_____

_____

_____

_____

_____

_____

THANK YOU

I first must give thanks to God, the Source of My Life. In God I move, live and have my being. Once I accepted that I was loved by this Divine Intelligence my life has never been the same. It is this Love that reminds me of the conversations we had before the beginning of time. Thank You!

I want thank my Mom and Dad for your continuous love and support. You are and have always been an example of what it is to be like God in the Earth. Your love for people, your integrity, and your wisdom will forever play a pivotal part in my life. I thank God that I chose You two to be my parents.

I want to thank my son, Justin, for being the loving son that are. You are just absolutely amazing! I am so honored to have been chosen by you to be Your mommy. Every day that I see You I am reminded just how blessed I am. I can't imagine what life would be like without you. I love You Shnuckums!

I want to thank my siblings (Karen, Carol, Valerie and Charles) my brothers-in-law (Delroy, Anthony and Walton) and my nieces and nephews (Amanda, Karryann, Brianna, Emilia, Courtney, Matthew, Kevin, Jason and Jullian) for loving me and always having my back. I know that no matter what I can count on all of You and you are always rooting for me. My family is amazing!

I want to thank Alethea and Janelle, for being the most amazing friends I have ever had. I am so grateful to have you both in my life. You are Beautiful and Powerful women and I am excited about your future!

I want to thank Dr. Undrai Fizer for being an incredible Spiritual Father and Mentor to me. Thank you for showing me the way and loving me through this journey back to me.

I want to thank Pastor Greg Stamper, Pastor Yolanda Batts and the Celebration Spiritual Center for being the answer to my prayers of a loving Church family that embodies the fullness of God, with no fear only love!

Last but not least, I want to thank Emmanuel for choosing me and loving me unconditionally. Thank you for always being a reminder to Me and Justin that "God is with Us". You are the answer to my prayers. I love you!

CPSIA information can be obtained
at www.ICGtesting.com
Printed in the USA
FFOW03n0244090117
31106FF